GUILLAUME CHEQUESPIERRE
AND THE OISE SALON

ARTIST: BEATRICE BAUMGARTNER

Guillaume Chèquespierre and the Oise Salon

AN ANTHOLOGY
SELECTED & EDITED BY

John Hulme

1817

HARPER & ROW, PUBLISHERS, New York
Cambridge, Philadelphia, San Francisco, Washington
London, Mexico City, São Paulo, Singapore, Sydney·

FIRST U.S. EDITION 1986

Designer: Kim Llewellyn

Library of Congress Cataloging-in-Publication Data
Hulme, John.
  Guillaume Chèquespierre and the Oise Salon.

  Homophonic verses written by John Hulme.
  Includes index.
  1. Macaronic literature.   2. Nonsense-verses.
I. Title.
PN1489.Z7H78   1986   841   86-45716
ISBN 0-06-015696-1

86 87 88 89 90 **MVP** 10 9 8 7 6 5 4 3 2 1

For Peter and Sarah

13, rue du Chat Mort

Foreword

I first came across the works of Guillaume Chèquespierre among the literary effects of my late benefactor Professor Dr. Gustav Leberwurst, during one of my prolonged visits to Strasbourg.[1] It was my research assistant, Mlle Beaucorps,[2] who drew my attention to the faded volumes, lying on a divan in one corner of the Professor's study-bedroom, and with her invaluable help I was able to piece together the history of the little band of writers who formed the Oise salon, and to select some of their poetic gems for inclusion in this book.

There are few, if any, references to the Oise poets in the standard histories of French literature, and even the house in which they met, in the Rue du Chat Mort, is not marked out in any way, except by the Louis XIV pissoir which stands outside the door. Not for them the fame of Vigny or of Hugo, but only the obscurity of the literary under-dog, or rather le sous-chien.

Their undoubted leader was Guillaume Chèquespierre, a prolific writer whose works include *"Messieurs Forts*

---

1. Readers of Mörder Guss Reims will need no further explanation.
2. I had been obliged to pension off Birgit, the Professor's former housekeeper, who had reached the age of 25.

Messieurs," a circus tale about a family of strong men; *"Rome
et Eau, Anjou Layette,"* a romantic novel which begins by
the fountains of Rome and ends with the birth of a baby in
the Loire Valley; and *"Jus Liasse Six Ares"* (*"A Wad of
Gravy for Six Acres"*), in which a Roman emperor sells his
birthright for a mess of pottage.

With his wife Anne, Chèquespierre left his native hamlet
of Stratte-Forte sur Avonne in the *département* of Oise in
1880 and settled in Paris. Here they founded a literary salon
to which they soon attracted a regular circle of minor poets
and other small[1] writers, many of them fellow exiles from the
Oise district. These included Jean Quittce, Guillaume Bléque,
Henri Longuevélo, Thomas Gris, A. Lefrette d'Énisonne,
Robert Brunenc, S. Colleriche, the mysterious A. Nonimousse
and others whose works appear in the following pages.
One who particularly stands out is the eccentric Guillaume
Veuseveute, whose unconventional behaviour earned him the
undisputed title of the Oise donkey.

The themes expressed in their poems are simple, often
homely: they write of eggs and of garlic, of water-butts and
pile-drivers, of donkeys and naiads, as they sing the praises of
their native Oise and dream of the "Golden Land."
Unfortunately their language and syntax are not always as
straightforward as one might wish, and so I have added a
number of explanatory footnotes to try to clarify the more
obscure passages, together with a glossary of proper names for
ease of reference.

---

1. See poems 10 and 11 for further details.

The poems should ideally be read aloud, as they were originally in the Oise salon a hundred years ago, preferably after eating liberal quantities of garlic to create an authentic atmosphere. Those who find pronunciation difficult should consult a dictionary. Those who find the footnotes helpful should consult a psychiatrist.

John Hulme

1

Tout pille or, note, tout pille, date hisse[1] de caisse tiens!
Où est d'air tisse n'eau bleue Inde mainte? Tous ouverts
De silence, Anne d'arrose offerte rageuse forte jaune
Or;[2] tout teck âme sagène,[3] c'est ta si oeuf trou bel ce.
Anne bâilleur pose en gaine d'aime.[4]

—G. CHÈQUESPIERRE

1 He fears that his gold is being pillaged and tells his wife to
"hoist" the date on the till. This expression and the reference to
the Indian Ocean in the next line reveal a nautical background.

2. All are gaping in silence, as the furious Anne has offered to
water down the strong yellow gold.

3. Old Russian measure, equivalent to just over two metres. He
says his soul is like a length of teak and as beautiful as an egg-hole.

4. Nevertheless she has no difficulty in getting the money from
her "beloved yawner" and putting it in her corsets.

2

Freine ce romance qu'un trime[1] haine, laine demi yeux
    hier ce.[2]
Ail comme tout béret[3] six ares note tout près cime
De Yves;[4] elle dattes mène d'où livres safre;[5] te sème
De gourdes, hisse oeuf tines tertre vite, d'air Beaune ce.[6]

—G. CHÈQUESPIERRE

1. To toil. The Muse had evidently deserted him.

2. Someone had half pulled the wool over his eyes on the
previous day.

3. "Old hat." He claims that there are six "ares" (nearly one-
seventh of an acre) of garlic near to Yves' summit.

4. Patron saint of lawyers (1253–1303); Feast Day 19th May.

5. It seems strange that she should take the dates and ignore the
pounds of sapphires.

6. She also plants gourds and hoists egg-casks quickly up a
hillock, in the manner of someone from Beaune. Albumen is
widely used in filtering and clarifying wine, but the part played
by gourds is less obvious.

3

Noue[1]—y ce devine! Terre oeuf ourdit,[2] ce corne teinte
M'aide clore rieuse; sous mer bâille, dise sonne oeuf
choc.[3]

....

Ah os! Ah os! Maille qui ne d'homme fourra os.[4]

—G. CHÈQUESPIERRE

1. A water-meadow or gutter tilo. Chèquespierre, enigmatic as
ever, challenges us to guess which.

2. "Hatched." Usually applied to plots rather than to eggs. He
claims that the horny tinge helps him to shut up the laughing
woman—Mme Chèquespierre was well known for her sense of
humour.

3. "If you laugh under water, you will ring with egg-shock."

4. "Oh bone! Oh bone! No stitch from a man shall stuff a bone."
A reference to the rag-and-bone trade, in which Chèquespierre
had served his apprenticeship before moving to Paris.

4

O suite de mots ne l'ail te se lippe serpent tisse bain que.[1]
Hyères[2] ville visite Anne lettre Saône[3] sauf musée que
Crépine[4] au rire ce; sauf cette île naissance naiade
Bec homme de duchesse oeuf souhaite âme honni.[5]

—G. CHÈQUESPIERRE

1. "A series of words with no garlic on the lip, while the serpent
is weaving a bath." An obscure expression.

2. Winter health resort in the Var, near Toulon.

3. River which flows into the Rhône at Lyons.

4. A fringe. Mme Chèquespierre apparently left out the museum
because it bordered on the ridiculous.

5. Apart from this island, the birth of a water-nymph with a beak
like a duchess's husband is said to make an egg wish its soul were
disgraced. Yet another example of Chèquespierre's enigmatic style.

5

Si ce rôt yole[1] trop neuf quine[2] ce, dix ceps[3] terre d'aieul.
Dessert touffe ma geste et décide oeuf masse.
Des auteur est daine de mies par à d'ail[4] ce
Dise fort tresse bile te; bâille née chère foreur salve
À gaine;[5] ce tine[6] vais Jean ânes de hante oeuf où or.

—G. CHÈQUESPIERRE

1. Roast skiff. This unusual dish is believed to have originated from the Vikings' habit of burning their boats.

2. A row of five numbers in a lottery.

3. Vine stocks or flap-mushrooms. If the roast skiff is too new, Chèquespierre advises the use of ten of these from ancestral soil. The quantity of eggs for the tufty dessert is optional.

4. Crumbs of doe in garlic. The reference to bile in the next line comes as no surprise.

5. His dearly-born wife yawns while the driller fires a salvo at her corsets.

6. A water-butt. John hopes to find golden eggs in it, but it is haunted by donkeys.

6

Ail où on d'air de l'aune, liasse à clou de.[1]
Date flot s'en aille or vèle sénile ce.[2]
Où en haut la douane saillit sauré croûte
À hausse t'oeuf gaule;[3] d'haine d'affût d'île ce.[4]

—G. VEUSEVEUTE

1. "There is garlic in the air near the alder tree, where a bundle of papers is nailed." French poets are notoriously partial to garlic, and Veuseveute was no exception. He often nailed his poems to trees.

2. "On the date when the wave (of garlic) goes away, this senile fellow will have a calf" (cf. to have kittens).

3. He describes how he leapt into the air at the Customs with a kippered crust and lifted someone's egg with a fishing rod.

4. "This island is a hated hiding place." Veuseveute's eccentric behaviour at the Customs earned him a two-year stretch on Devil's Island.

7

Art phallique, art phallique, art phallique en ouate![1]
Or Lin[2] de va lit oeuf dettes, rôde de sexe; un d'arrête
For ouate; de l'ail te Brie gai de.[3]
Char je fort de gonze[4] y s'aide.
Indu de va lit oeuf dettes, rôde de sexe, un d'arrête.[5]

—A. D'ÉNISONNE

1. D'Énisonne was a strongly puritanical man who felt that
modern art was corrupting the cottonwool minds of the public.

2. Saint Lin, Pope from 64 to 76. He is accused of going to bed
with egg debts, while sex is on the prowl.

3. "One has been arrested by the cottonwool tribunal; even your
Brie is gay with garlic."

4. "Bloke." He would put them in a strong waggon and let every
man look out for himself.

5. He repeats his complaint that it is wrong to go to bed with egg
debts while sex is on the prowl and yet only one person has been
arrested—probably Veuseveute.

8

De chez de sauf n'ailles-te ou air folie ne farce te.[1]
À ce trou anal[2] paille ne vie l'âge pas ce te
Et y où sous bord[3] mie de ce n'eau âne d'ail ce
À bain heure[4] vite de se traîne-je de va y ce.
Aix[5] elle si hors!

——H. LONGUEVÉLO

1. "Unless you leave home, your madness will not be funny."

2. A medical expression. He says it is the last straw, at his time
of life.

3. "Underboard" (cf. overboard).

4. "Bath time." He calls him a garlic donkey—an epithet
frequently applied to Veuseveute—and drags himself off quickly.

5. Presumably Aix-les-Bains. His wife has to wait outside, mixed
bathing being forbidden under Prefectorial Decree no. 46 of 12th
May 1833.

9

De Oise à noter beau y.[1]
Âne à noter beau y, vas-y![2]
Iran et ouais![3] Tousse côte lande
De pipe elle fort; tousse-y![4]

—J. QUITTCE

1. "It is nice to note things about Oise." This *département* consists
of Picardy and part of the Ile-de-France. Its attractions include
the cathedral of Beauvais, with its magnificent 13th Century choir.

2. "There is a notable donkey there—go ahead!" A scarcely veiled
reference to the eccentric Veuseveute.

3. "My word!" He expresses surprise that a female pipe-smoker
in Iran should cough so strongly on the sandy moorland.

4. "Cough away!" Not a charitable remark.

10

Âne dite dose fi tine;[1] haine chênes taille me
Où hors coupon[2] haine glande; ce Montaigne[3] se gris ne,
Âne d'Oise de haut lit, l'âme oeuf gode.
Y naine glande ce plaie sainte pas ce tierce scie ne.[4]

—G. BLÉQUE

1. He was called a donkey for taking a dose from the shameful water-butt.

2. He hates the size of oak trees where his hate gland is "beyond the ticket."

3. French moralist (1533–1592) immortalized by his Essays. It is true that he does not grow grey, but there is no reason to call him a Oise donkey from a high bed with a soul like a crumpled egg. In any case he was born in Périgord, which is nowhere near Oise, so this is more likely to be another reference to Veuseveute.

4. "This holy wound does not saw one third off his dwarf gland" (cf. "Thyroid Deficiencies in Certain Minor Poets"—*Journal Médical Français* 1889, Vol. XIII).

11

O. .ouate[1] cannelle dîne ail, tâte âme ce
À l'eau; nain pèle lit, l'oeil terrine
Dessèche;[2] hisse oui d'air de fronde lait que
Anneau berce zinc.[3]

—J. QUITTCE

1. A cryptic reference to Veuseveute. He is said to dine on
cinnamon and garlic while searching his soul by the water—
presumably during his stretch on Devil's Island.

2. "The dwarf strips his bed with one eye on the dish which is
drying up." For further details of Veuseveute's height cf. the
previous poem, Note 4.

3. He hoists milk in the air and slings it around, then sends
(them) to sleep with a zinc ring. The first part of this sounds
typical of Veuseveute's unconventional behaviour, but the
reference to his hypnotic powers is not confirmed by any other
source.

12

Hie[1] toise[2] de ce coup n'air espère russe
Dattes celtes[3] de, oui ne terre y si
Âne[4] de ce qui père a de teck anise[5] lit, tel dort terre.
Tout ber[6] rime comme pain ni.

—H. LONGUEVÉLO

1. A pile-driver, earth-rammer or paviour's beetle.

2. An ancient measure of length equal to 1.949 metres.

3. He must not hope to learn Russian all at once from eating Celtic dates.

4. He is a donkey because his father has a teak bed, like people who sleep on the ground.

5. An umbelliferous plant with aromatic seeds used for curing flatulence (cf. the next poem, Note 5).

6. A launching cradle or boiler seating. He says that it never rhymes with bread.

13

Huile chou ou or?[1] Qu'à l'itou[2] face terre
S'aida ouaille[3] tine; tu as ce n'aile
D'air ça, port pousse close bée;[4] Indus[5]
Anise très dîne, en mailles t'aile.[6]

—L. CAROLLE

1. "Cabbage oil or gold?"

2. Also (Old French *hel* from Latin *hic talis*).

3. A member of a flock. Faced with the above question and also with the ground, he helped himself from a water-butt. Another reference to the strange behaviour of Veuseveute.

4. He complains about someone's lack of wings and talks of pushing a gaping enclosure into the harbour.

5. Large river in Pakistan, where he claims that a lot of aniseed is eaten (cf. the previous poem, Note 5).

6. "He is in stitches about your wing." Members of flocks do not qualify for wings (or harps) as long as they are earthbound, so his amusement is in bad taste.

14

Gâteur y est rosse[1] boude ce ouaille le y est mais
Eau la taille mise cette île oeuf l'ail[2] Inn.[3]
Anne dise sème flou air dattes semelles;[4] ce tout dés.[5]
Tue moraux ou île bée d'ail Inn.[6]

—R. ERRIQUE

1. An objectionable person who spoils everything and falls out with the rest of the flock. Almost certainly Veuseveute, especially in view of the next line.

2. Garlic egg. This was the standard continental breakfast on Devil's Island.

3. A tributary of the Danube.

4. Mme Chèquespierre told him to sow dates in the hazy air, with his soles.

5. "All dice"—i.e., a matter of luck.

6. He should kill his scruples, or the island will be gaping with garlic from the River Inn.

15

Terrine que tout mie eau ne lie;[1] vite taille n'ail ce
Anne d'ail huile plaide-je vite;[2] maille ne
Hors livre à qui ce butine[3] soucoupe.
Âne d'ail[4] le note loup que fort ouaille ne.

—B. JEANSONNE

1. "Water will not thicken a pot full of crumbs." An old Oise
proverb.

2. He pleads with Mme Chèquespierre not to sharpen the garlic
but to bring it quickly with some oil.

3. To plunder. "Don't take a stitch from the book of the man who
looted the saucer." Could this have been Veuseveute?

4. Such terms as "the garlic donkey" and "the noted wolf who was
only a strong sheep" confirm the suspicion that it was indeed
Veuseveute.

16

Seau huile Gounod;[1] Moreau[2] rôt vine
Seau lait teins-tu de naiade
D'odeur art te bis[3] t'île as le vine
Âne démon[4] bis t'île as brailles-te.[5]

—LAURE DE BAILLERONNE

1. Charles (1818–1893), French composer famous for his operas and religious works.

2. Gustave (1826–1898), post-impressionist artist. In this scene one has a bucketful of oil while the other adds alcohol to the roast and stains a water-nymph with a bucket of milk. Evidently some kind of artistic "happening."

3. French for "encore" (cf. *impasse*, which is French for "cul-de-sac").

4. "The demon donkey." Who else but Veuseveute?

5. He tells him to bawl again on his island, as he is such an ace at it.

17

Jaune qu'il peine Oise air;[1] si tisane
Oeuf craie[2] dite Anne rit n'a ou ne,
À traîne bain de képi Taine[3] y que vas-y!
Qeuf fée mousse,[4] l'on donne ta ou ne.

—G. COUPEUR

1. Thanks to the introduction of smokeless fuels in 1957, the *département* of Oise is no longer troubled by yellow air as it was when this poem was written.

2. An infusion of egg and chalk sounds unlikely to help, and it was no wonder that Mme Chèquespierre laughed.

3. Hippolyte (1828–1893), French philosopher, critic and historian. He is said to have worn a peaked cap while dragging a bath, an improbable story which is far more likely to refer to Veuseveute.

4. Fairy egg mousse. This can be eaten hot, as an *hors d'oeuvre*, or served *glacé* as a dessert.

18

Y âne qui doux d'elle qu'aime tout ta ou ne
Raille;[1] dîne on à pot[2] ni.
Stuc à fée[3] terrine y satin,
Colle dite ma carreau ni.[4]

—E. BANQUES

1. A tale of unrequited love. The so-called donkey (could this be
Veuseveute yet again?) was sweet on her, but she had other
admirers and made fun of him.

2. To take pot luck. Apparently she never did.

3. "Fairy stucco." This style of decoration, so popular in the
Second Empire, is rarely found nowadays.

4. She stood her dishes on satin and claimed that they never stuck
to the tiles.

19

Chou art[1] rôle de phare d'air, oui l'y aime, de y'on mince aide.

Agneau air aspic,[2] homme verre y où ailles-te?[3]

Anne y êtes, jus y ne c'est sainte lisse, tante agneau raide.[4]

D'où y où signe qu'à t'y ou régie tisse railles-te?[5]

—L. CAROLLE

1. Cabbage artistry. He sees himself in the role of an airy lighthouse lending a little help to cabbage lovers.

2. A dish consisting of clear, savoury meat jelly and containing fowl, game or fish, etc.—in this case, lamb.

3. He wonders where the man is going with his glass.

4. He tells Mme Chèquespierre that the gravy is not as blessedly smooth as it should be, and that his aunt is stiff from eating the lamb. A clear case of salmonella poisoning.

5. "Is this a sign that you are weaving to mock the management?"

20

Eau tout pie en haine glande.[1]
Noeud date est prèle[2] ce d'air
Âne d'où est ver; où Aix[3] en haine glande
Sise Somme morne haine un où air.
Date ce l'eau est[4] beau sonde bruche[5] voûte; chiffre
Ronde de elle me tripot;[6] la reine taille ni l'if.[7]

—R. BRUNENC

1. "Put pious water in your hate gland." A truly noble exhortation.

2. Horse-tail, a genus of cryptogamous plants. He has tied a knot
in it to remind himself of the date for airing the donkey, which
has worms.

3. Aix-les-Bains, a spa in Savoy. The air may well be good for
spleen, but Aix is definitely not situated on the "gloomy Somme."

4. The East (cf. the Gare de l'Est in Paris).

5. A weevil or pea-beetle. When the eastern water is calm
someone looks for them in the vault.

6. "In round figures, she is fiddling about with me."

7. A yew-tree, taper-hearse or draining-rack. Whichever it is, the
Queen never prunes it.

21

Comines[1] de mer craie de lucarnes bigarre.[2]
Indigne dite comme de se traîne gestes fille guère.[3]
Hisse cuir l'on côte front;[4] mille toux aident![5]
Oise ares fauves y est l'eau, un d'ares fauves raide.[6]

—R. BRUNENC

1. Small town on the River Lys, near Lille. The reference to the sea-side must be ascribed to poetic licence or to Brunenc's appalling ignorance of geography. See also the previous poem, in which he locates Aix-les-Bains on the River Somme.

2. The town mottles its attic windows with chalk (cf. *The Decorative Use of Brownstone on Door-Steps in Oswaldtwistle,* ed. H. Ramsbotham, 1929).

3. "The girl scarcely deserved to be accused of dragging her movements."

4. "Leather is hoisted on the coast." See Note 1.

5. "May a thousand coughs help me!" (cf. *Mille pardons!*).

6. He recalls the fawn-coloured acres of Oise, where the water is, and says that someone from there is stiff—probably a reference to Carolle's aunt (see Poem 19, Note 4).

22

Où or terre, où or terre?[1] Et verre y où air?
De verre y bord de ce dite serine[2] que.
Où or terre, où or terre?[3] Et verre y où air?
Nord haine y d'Europe tù terrine que.[4]

—S. COLLERICHE

1. The quest for the "Golden Land" inspired many of the poets in the Oise salon, and there are references to it in the works of Colleriche, Bléque, Longuevélo and others.

2. A female canary. Colleriche trained it to sit on the edge of his glass and cry for air.

3. The "Golden Land" again. Another poet, Brunenc, twice took his holidays on the Côte d'Or under the impression that he was going to the "Golden Land," or at least to the sea-side (but cf. the previous poem, Note 1, for an assessment of his geographical knowledge).

4. As a North European he has a hatred of potted meat.

23

O mise tresses mailles ne!^{1} Où air are^2 yu^3 rot mine
Ose dé Inde hier yeux trou louve;^{4} ce Comines
Datte canne scie ne que beau taillant l'eau
Tripes^5 n'eau feutre prêté ce oui tine
Dieu n'est Seine dîne Louvre ce mie tine.
Effarée où ail ce mince, sans dot nos.^{6}

—G. CHÈQUESPIERRE

1. "Don't put your locks in stitches!"—i.e., keep your hair on.

2. One *are* equals about four poles.

3. Chinese measure of capacity.

4. He is urged to gamble on an eructating mine in India where
he had seen a female wolf's hole the day before.

5. Comines is not particularly noted for its tripe. The unusual
recipe given here involves some date-cane sawn with a fine
cutting-edge, some borrowed felt without water, an ungodly Seine
dinner and a museum cask full of crumbs.

6. The girl is frightened that the garlic is too scanty and that they
will lose their dowry.

Tailles guerre,[1] tailles guerre, beurre naine brailles-te[2]
Un deux foreuse; t'oeuf de n'ailles-te?
ou ôter mort ta lande or ail.[3]
Coude frais[4] me taille fière foule si; mettre-y![5]

——G. BLÉQUE

1. "War waists." A popular name for the Paris fashions during the 1870–71 siege (cf. "to tighten one's belt").

2. To brawl. A female dwarf arguing over some butter is compared to a drilling machine.

3. He wishes she would go away with her egg, or that death would take her off to her "heathland of golden garlic"—presumably the Côte d'Or, whose gastronomic delights include snails in garlic butter.

4. "Cool elbow." A slightly warmer version of the cold shoulder.

5. "Put it there!" She says that she is proud of her waist-line in any crowd and invites him to shake on it.

25

Lit si bord d'haine tout canne Aix.[1]
Anne gai faire moutard[2] fort tille[3] où Aix
Où haine chez sort ouate chez hâte donne
Chez gais faire fard[4] d'air fort Taiwan.[5]

—A. NONIMOUSSE

1. "If you hate the edge of your bed, get a cane one from Aix."
Neither Aix-les-Bains (a health resort) nor Aix-en-Provence
(soap, oil, almonds) is particularly noted for the manufacture of
beds. Could this be Aix-la-Chapelle (textile industry, machines,
needles)?

2. A kid or brat. No connection with mustard.

3. Bast, bass, a cuddy or a (cooper's) adze. The last one sounds
most likely.

4. Make-up. He hates home so he gets out the cottonwool and
hastily makes up to go and visit some gay friends.

5. Japanese name for the island of Formosa.

Esther sème ce eau le veule d'eau verre.[1]
Esther port ouate guette ce de blême.[2]
Esther rit chouettes guette ce de plaie jour.[3]
Est-ce haine titre et bleue mine, chai[4] me.

—A. NONIMOUSSE

1. Esther spreads water from a pale water glass. From her actions later in the poem she appears to be a Customs official, so the water may be illicit *eau-de-vie.*

2. She watches out for cottonwool at the ghastly port. It would be interesting to know which French harbour earned this description and what was hidden in the cottonwool.

3. She laughs as she lies in wait for wounded owls by day. The import of livestock was, of course, subject to strict controls, and owls were no exception whether wounded or not.

4. A storehouse for wines and spirits. She ponders on her hated title, but consoles herself that her storehouse is a "blue mine."

27

Comment? Tout de gare daines mortes?
Fort de blague!¹ Battent naiades as flots ne.²
Comment? Tout de gare daines mortes?
Ail émir à deux gais talons.³

—A. D'ÉNISONNE

1. He refuses to believe that the whole railway station is full of
dead docs, and dismisses this as a load of bunkum.

2. "The ace water-nymphs cannot beat the waves." Naiads were
freshwater nymphs, so they were not faced with waves of any
great size. They certainly had no difficulty with Hylas, the servant
of Hercules, because all that was ever found of him was his empty
water-jug.

3. He describes the story about the dead does as a load of garlic
fit for an Arab prince with two gay heels. An unusual metaphor.

28

Chat l'ail[1] comme paires six touez sous mer ce thé.
Saoul hâte mort;[2] l'oeuf lianes mort thème paraître,
Rouf oins doux chèque;[3] ce dart lion boudes oeuf mais
Anne sous mer;[4] ce liasse atoll touche or tous dés.[5]

—G. CHÈQUESPIERRE

1. Cat-garlic—an unusually pungent species widely used in Oise cooking (cf. *ratatouille à la mode de Beauvais, bouillabaisse à la mode de Compiègne*, etc.). This recipe for making garlic tea states that six pairs of cloves should be towed under water.

2. "The glutton is hastening his death." A salutary note.

3. The subject of egg on tropical creepers appears to be dead, so he suggests a quiet cheque to "oil the deck-house."

4. "This lion sting has gone off eggs, but Anne is under water." Presumably towing cloves.

5. "This bundle of coral islands is striking gold at every throw of the dice." Chèquespierre's imagination was stronger than his knowledge of geology.

29

Bellot, bellot saoul vine terre;[1] vingt
Sous hâte notes seau un quinte
À ce mince Ingres[2] t'étude.
Taille toute hisse notes seau, qui ne
Bec ose, sous hâte notes;[3] scie ne
Hors le seau taille bref[4]—Beyrouth![5]

—G. CHÈQUESPIERRE

1. A dapper drunk is told to add alcohol to the earth—a neat way
of avoiding a certain coarse expression.

2. Jean-Auguste-Dominic (1780–1867), a classical painter much
influenced by Raphael. Someone is offered 20 sous to hasten to
this slim artist with a bucketful of fifth notes from a musical work.

3. He is to hoist up the whole size of the bucketful of notes, not
daring to open his mouth, and then hurry off with the sous and
the notes.

4. He is not to saw pieces out of the bucket because of its brief
size.

5. Capital of the Lebanon. Ingres painted several portraits of
odalisques.

30

Orle de veule sasse[1] tais-je
Âne hors le domaine inoui mène; mire[2] lit plaît heuse[3]
Thé hâve, d'air excite, sain d'air entraîne; cesse
Anne![4] Où on Menin[5] hisse taille me plaît ce mène y
   pâte ce.

—G. CHÈQUESPIERRE

1. A flabby bailing-scoop with a heraldic inset border. He agrees
to keep it a secret and leads a donkey out of an unheard-of estate.

2. A surveyor's pole.

3. Mediaeval leggings. He likes to wear them in bed while
drinking weak tea in an exciting fashion, with a healthy air which
carries him away.

4. An aside to Mme Chèquespierre.

5. Town in Belgium on the River Lys. He likes the way they
have hoisted their waists and asks for some paste to be taken there.
The significance of this request is not clear.

Et toi, ce Louvre un dise lasse.[1]
Vite hé Inde eau, Inde hé—non, ni nos![2]
Date or de gril[3] ne corne fil ce dite pas ce.
En d'aspirine taille me, de eau ne l'y pris terrine
   taille me.
Où haine boeuf ce doux zinc est digne, digne dîne.[4]
Souhaite Louvre ce l'oeuf d'aspirine.[5]

—G. CHÈQUESPIERRE

1. Museums can be very tiring.

2. There is some confusion as he calls for tonic water.

3. He is on the grill (the rack, tenterhooks) and cannot find the thread with his feelers.

4. "Cut me an aspirin, don't take any water, cut me an earthenware dish. Where there is hatred of beef, this gentle zinc is worthy to dine off." Quite a bad case of museum-mania.

5. He wishes the Louvre had an aspirin the size of an egg— though it is doubtful whether even this would help him, at this late stage.

32

Bâille de chose oeuf guichet[1] gourmet.
Bâille de chaîne y ne bigue si où or terre.[2]
Ce tout de ce oui Guam[3] oeuf nos commises.
Dort terre oeuf démon, nos commises.[4]

—H. LONGUEVÉLO

1. A booking-office window. Railway omelettes make this food inspector yawn.

2. He also yawns at chains if there is no derrick from the golden land.

3. The main island of the Marianas Archipelago in the North Pacific; products include maize, sweet potatoes and bananas; population (1960) 67,044. Apparently some female clerks had sent an egg from there.

4. According to these clerks, there was a devil of an egg asleep on the ground. Possibly an obscure reference to Omelette, a Humpty-Dumpty-like character created by Chèquespierre in a play of the same name.

33

Veine ail six culs cinq;[1] bâille de où orle[2]
Antique de chez perte;[3] bellot si ce n'aile
Ante[4] homme berce l'orque[5] si ne tout dehors le
Ânes mille comme ce féroce haine eau mine pelle.

—G. CHÈQUESPIERRE

1. "The vein of garlic was six bottoms by five." A primitive
measure of area which clearly pre-dates the metric system

2. A border on an escutcheon, set in from the edge. He yawns at
such antiques.

3. The lost property office.

4. The handle of a paintbrush.

5. A grampus, or orc.

In this poem, Chèquespierre depicts a dapper man with a wingless
paintbrush handle cradling a grampus, or orc, while all outside a
thousand donkeys are shovelling water out of a mine with
ferocious hatred. Grampuses, or orcs, cannot survive long out of
water.

34

Tue moraux, Anne, tue moraux, Anne, tue moraux![1]
Crêpes synthèses petit pèse, frondez tous dés.[2]
Tuteur lasse si la belle offre cor dettes, thème
Anne d'or lourd;[3] yeuse te dé sève, l'ail t'aide foule ce.[4]
Ce ouais! Tout d'usité dettes; haute, haute, prive
    Cannes d'elles.[5]

—G. CHÈQUESPIERRE

1. He urges his wife to kill her morals.

2. He wants her to make synthetic pancakes and to give short weight, slinging all the dice in the process.

3. If the beautiful one is tired and offers her guardian an antler for her debts, Mme Chèquespierre is to mention the topic of the heavy gold.

4. "Your die is covered in sap from the holly-oak, but the garlic will help you in this crowd." A sound piece of advice.

5. He is surprised at all his current debts and decides it is high time he ridded Cannes of them. The reference is to Cannes-sur-Avonne (Oise), where Chèquespierre was a regular visitor to the casino.

35

On aille de saillies,[1] dérive air l'ail.
L'on que file[2] c'oeuf Bali, Anne d'oeuf raille.
Date Claude de volt âne mites[3] de ce qu'ail,
Anne trous de file ce de rôde ronces bâille.
Tout mène y toux air de camelote.[4]

—A. D'ÉNISONNE

1. Leaps and bounds. The garlic is so strong that it turns the air
to one side.

2. To palm. Whoever palmed this Indonesian egg was being
funny, according to Mme Chèquespierre.

3. Donkey-mites. While Claude tries to exterminate them—by the
use of electricity or garlic—she yawns holes as she prowls after
him through the brambles.

4. Rubbish, trash. The air is so bad that it makes everyone cough.
All in all, this seems to have been a rather unpleasant outing.

36

En ça, ne doux dite coup belle la Cannes.
As tête, lippe l'azur d'homme, dit cri
Où air;[1] alfa[2] de sais crête riverain.
Truc à Verne[3] ce, mais jure l'esse[4] tout main.
Don[5] toux à sonne l'esse, si . . .

—S. COLLERICHE

1. "It was no soft coup that the so-called beauty brought off at Cannes. Her head was ace, but her bottom lip was blue like a man's and she was crying for air." Tight-lacing was the downfall of many a Victorian beauty on both sides of the Channel.

2. Esparto grass. He knows that she got it from the crest by the river.

3. Jules (1828–1905), French novelist.

4. An S-shaped hook, linchpin or sound-hole of a violin, etc. Colleriche says this was one of Verne's tricks, but he swears that the S-shaped hook or whatever was in his hand all the time.

5. "He had a talent for coughing and making the S-shaped hook etc. ring."

37

De coeur fille où tôle[1] ce de n'elle oeuf patine dais
De l'eau; an gourde oins ce l'eau lit hors delit.[2]
Déploiement eau m'Oise[3] pelotes six ou y ri ouais![4]
En livres ce de veule tout d'Arc[5] naissante tout mi.

—T. GRIS

1. Sheet metal. She has hardened her heart but he compares her to an egg skating on a canopy over the water.

2. He has been oiling a gourd for the past year, lying on a water bed and not taking offence.

3. The river rises in the Ardennes and flows into the Seine at Conflans-Sainte-Honorine, near Versailles. This "spreading out of the water" is a reference to the great flood of March 1847.

4. He is surprised that six balls of wool should cause such amazement.

5. The Maid of Orléans was captured at Compiègne and tried by the Bishop of Beauvais—hence her connection with the *département* of Oise. He says that in books she is shown as a flabby character who is only half born.

38

De peuple se fêles[1] de fer où elles tout de chez de.
Un deux oui soupirants[2] sondent oeuf de coule
  colonne aide
De veine; ce bellot nos l'on guerre ânes cinquaine;[3]
  délivre ce
Noix ruse anise bout, somme—d'air;[4] y mage rit
  cive ce.[5]

—G. COUPEUR

1. To crack. The iron will of the nations is cracking wherever all
the women are leaving home (cf. *The Decline of Family Life in
the Eighties* by G. Coupeur, Paris 1885).

2. Suitors. They are always testing eggs and slipping behind
pillars, helped on by luck.

3. "This dapper man is one of our war donkeys from the fifties."
In the Crimean War the French Army relied heavily on donkeys
because of the shortage of horses.

4. "He delivers nuts by trickery and pieces of aniseed, in short—
air."

5. "The Magus laughs at this civet cat."

39

De quoi litée oeuf merci;[1] hisse note se traîne de
Hie[2] trop père, tasse de gêne, telle reine forme évent.
Ah bon! Ce plaise bénite, et tisse toise;[3] blesse te
État blesse thème date, gui vesce intime, dattes teck ce.[4]

—G. CHÈQUESPIERRE

1. He is grateful for the egg, whatever litter it is from.

2. A pile-driver. He runs up a signal saying that his father is
dragging it too far and making things difficult for a cup with the
Queen's shape on. This was probably a souvenir of the coronation
of Napoléon III and the Empress Eugénie.

3. He prays that the mug will be consecrated and weaves a device
for measuring conscripts.

4. "This historic topic harms the state like a deep-rooted tare in
mistletoe, or like dates in teak."

40

Où on ce Maure un tout de Brie je dire freine ce,[1] où
   on ce Maure
Orgue l'ose d'où or loupe,[2] oui ce urine[3] cliche dettes
Hie ne pisse[3] terre; ce noeud tine[4] sobre comme ce main,
À ce modiste cette île naissante hue[5] militée.

—G. CHÈQUESPIERRE

1. He calls for a halt to the import of North African cheese.

2. To botch or bungle. The Moors are daring to send organs from
where they mishandle gold.

3. Chèquespierre's language shows the strength of his feelings on
this matter, as he accuses them of stereotyping their debts with a
pile-driver.

4. A knot in a water-butt.

5. "Boo" or "Gee up." It is not clear which of these the newly-
born militated island is addressing to the milliner who is as sober
as a hand.

This poem is typical of the pessimism of Chèquespierre's later
years, which culminated in his swan-song *À Jus L'ail Quitte*
("The Garlic's Going Out of the Gravy").

English Translations

1. To be, or not to be: that is the question:
   Whether 'tis nobler in the mind to suffer
   The slings and arrows of outrageous fortune,
   Or to take arms against a sea of troubles,
   And by opposing end them?

   HAMLET III,i,56

2. Friends, Romans, countrymen, lend me your ears;
   I come to bury Caesar, not to praise him.
   The evil that men do lives after them,
   The good is oft interred with their bones.

   JULIUS CAESAR III,ii,79

3. Now is the winter of our discontent
   Made glorious summer by this sun of York

   . . . .

   A horse! A horse! My kingdom for a horse!

   KING RICHARD the THIRD V,iv,7

4. How sweet the moonlight sleeps upon this bank!
   Here we will sit, and let the sounds of music
   Creep in our ears: soft stillness and the night
   Become the touches of sweet harmony.

   THE MERCHANT OF VENICE V,i,54

5. This royal throne of kings, this sceptered isle,
   This earth of majesty, this seat of Mars,
   This other Eden, demi-paradise,
   This fortress built by Nature for herself
   Against infection and the hand of war.

   RICHARD II II,i,40

6. I wandered lonely as a cloud
   That floats on high o'er vales and hills,
   When all at once I saw a crowd,
   A host, of golden daffodils.

   DAFFODILS
   William Wordsworth

7. Half a league, half a league,
   Half a league onward,
   All in the valley of death
   Rode the six hundred.

   . . . .

   Forward the light brigade
   Charge for the guns he said.
   Into the valley of death
   Rode the six hundred.

   THE CHARGE OF THE LIGHT
   BRIGADE, St. 1 & 2
   Alfred, Lord Tennyson

8. The shades of night were falling fast,
   As through an Alpine village passed
   A youth, who bore, mid snow and ice,
   A banner with the strange device,
   Excelsior!

   EXCELSIOR
   H. W. Longfellow

9. There was a naughty boy
   And a naughty boy was he!
   He ran away to Scotland
   The people for to see!

   A SONG ABOUT MYSELF
   John Keats

10. And did those feet in ancient time
    Walk upon England's mountains green?
    And was the holy Lamb of God
    On England's pleasant pastures seen?

    Prefatory poem to MILTON
    (Jerusalem)
    William Blake

11. O, what can ail thee, knight-at-arms,
Alone and palely loitering?
The sedge has withered from the lake,
And no birds sing!

> LA BELLE DAME SANS MERCI St. 1
> John Keats

12. It was the schooner Hesperus,
That sailed the wintry sea;
And the skipper had taken his little daughter
To bear him company.

> THE WRECK OF THE HESPERUS
> H. W. Longfellow

13. "Will you walk a little faster?" said a whiting to a snail,
"There's a porpoise close behind us, and he's treading on my
tail."

> THE LOBSTER QUADRILLE St. 1
> Lewis Carroll

14. Gather ye rosebuds while ye may,
Old Time is still a-flying
And this same flower that smiles today
Tomorrow will be dying.

> TO THE VIRGINS TO MAKE MUCH
> OF TIME
> Robert Herrick

15. Drink to me only with thine eyes,
And I will pledge with mine;
Or leave a kiss but in the cup
And I'll not look for wine.

> TO CELIA St. 1
> Ben Jonson

16. So we'll go no more a-roving
So late into the night,
Though the heart be still as loving,
And the moon be still as bright.

> SO WE'LL GO NO MORE A 'ROVING
> George Gordon, Lord Byron

17. John Gilpin was a citizen
    Of credit and renown,
    A train-band captain eke was he
    Of famous London town.

    HISTORY OF JOHN GILPIN i
    William Cowper

18. Yankee Doodle came to town
    Riding on a pony,
    Stuck a feather in his hat
    And called it macaroni.

    ANONYMOUS

19. "You are old, Father William," the young man said,
    "And your hair has become very white;
    And yet you incessantly stand on your head—
    Do you think, at your age, it is right?"

    ALICE'S ADVENTURES IN
    WONDERLAND
    Lewis Carroll

20. Oh, to be in England now that April's there,
    And whoever wakes in England sees, some morning, unaware,
    That the lowest boughs and the brushwood sheaf
    Round the elm tree bole are in tiny leaf,

    HOME THOUGHTS FROM ABROAD
    Robert Browning

21. "Come in!" the Mayor cried, looking bigger
    And in did come the strangest figure!
    His queer long coat from heel to head
    Was half of yellow and half of red;

    THE PIED PIPER OF HAMELIN
    Robert Browning

22. Water, water, everywhere,
    The very boards did shrink.
    Water, water, everywhere
    Nor any drop to drink.

    THE ANCIENT MARINER St. 9
    S. T. Coleridge

23. O, mistress mine! Where are you roaming?
    O! Stay and hear; your true love's coming,
    That can sing both high and low.
    Trip no further, pretty sweeting;
    Journeys end in lovers meeting,
    Every wise man's son doth know.

                        TWELFTH NIGHT II,iii,42

24. Tiger, tiger, burning bright
    In the forests of the night,
    What immortal hand or eye
    Could frame thy fearful symmetry?

                        THE TIGER
                        William Blake

25. Lizzie Borden took an axe
    And gave her mother forty whacks;
    When she saw what she had done
    She gave her father forty-one!

                        Popular rhyme after the murder
                        trial of Lizzie Borden, Fall River,
                        Massachusetts, June 1893

26. It's the same the whole world over,
    It's the poor wot gets the blame,
    It's the rich wot gets the pleasure
    Isn't it a bloomin' shame?

                        Song, circa 1915

27. Come into the garden, Maud,
    For the black bat, night, has flown,
    Come into the garden, Maud,
    I am here at the gate alone.

                        MAUD xxii, St. 1
                        Alfred, Lord Tennyson

28. Shall I compare thee to a summer's day?
    Thou art more lovely and more temperate:
    Rough winds do shake the darling buds of May,
    And summer's lease hath all too short a date.

                        Sonnet 18, 1.i.ff.

29. Blow, blow thou winter wind!
    Thou art not so unkind
    As man's ingratitude;
    Thy tooth is not so keen,
    Because thou art not seen,
    Although thy breath be rude.

                                    AS YOU LIKE IT II,vii,174

30. All the world's a stage
    And all the men and women merely players:
    They have their exits and their entrances;
    And one man in his time plays many parts

                                    AS YOU LIKE IT II,vii.139

31. It was a lover and his lass,
    With a hey, and a ho, and a hey nonino,
    That o'er the green corn-field did pass,
    In the spring time, the only pretty ring time,
    When birds do sing, hey ding a ding ding;
    Sweet lovers love the spring.

                                    AS YOU LIKE IT V,iii,18

32. By the shores of Gitche Gumee,
    By the shining Big-Sea-Water,
    Stood the wigwam of Nokomis
    Daughter of the moon Nokomis

                                THE SONG OF HIAWATHA III
                                H. W. Longfellow

33. When icicles hang by the wall,
    And Dick the shepherd blows his nail,
    And Tom bears logs into the hall,
    And milk comes frozen home in pail,

                                    LOVE'S LABOUR'S LOST V,ii,920

34. Tomorrow, and tomorrow, and tomorrow,
    Creeps in this petty pace from day to day,
    To the last syllable of recorded time;
    And all our yesterdays have lighted fools
    The way to dusty death. Out, out, brief candle!

                                    MACBETH V,v,17

35. On either side the river lie
    Long fields of barley and of rye,
    That clothe the wold and meet the sky;
    And thro' the field the road runs by
    To many-towered Camelot.

    THE LADY OF SHALOTT i
    Alfred, Lord Tennyson

36. In Xanadu did Kubla Khan
    A stately pleasure-dome decree;
    Where Alph, the sacred river, ran
    Through caverns measureless to man
    Down to a sunless sea.

    KUBLA KHAN
    S. T. Coleridge

37. The curfew tolls the knell of parting day,
    The lowing herd winds slowly o'er the lea,
    The ploughman homeward plods his weary way,
    And leaves the world to darkness and to me.

    ELEGY WRITTEN IN A COUNTRY
    CHURCHYARD i
    Thomas Gray

38. The poplars are felled, farewell to the shade,
    And the whispering sound of the cool colonnade,
    The winds play no longer and sing in the leaves,
    Nor Ouse on his bosom their image receives.

    THE POPLAR FIELD
    William Cowper

39. The quality of mercy is not strained,
    It droppeth as the gentle rain from heaven
    Upon the place beneath; it is twice blessed.
    It blesseth him that gives and him that takes:

    THE MERCHANT OF VENICE
    IV,i,184

40. Once more unto the breach, dear friends, once more;
    Or close the wall up with our English dead!
    In peace there's nothing so becomes a man
    As modest stillness and humility:

HENRY V III,i,1

Index of First Lines

Seau huile Gounod; Moreau rôt vine · 16
Si ce rôt yole trop neuf quine ce · 5
Tailles guerre, tailles guerre, beurre naine brailles-te · 24
Terrine que tout mie eau ne lie; vite taille n'ail ce · 15
Tout pille or, note, tout pille · 1
Tue moraux, Anne, tue moraux, Anne, tue moreaux! · 34
Veine ail six culs cinq; bâille de où orle · 33
Y âne qui doux d'elle · 18

Glossary of Proper Names

Bibliography

L'Oise Gastronomique—A. Chèquespierre, 1881
Les Vins de l'Oise—G. Chèquespierre, 1882
Les Grands Vins de l'Oise—G. Chèquespierre, 1883
Les Plus Grands Vins de l'Oise—G. Chèquespierre, 1884
A Guide to Devil's Island—G. Veuseveute, 1885
The Oise Book of Garlic—A. Chèquespierre, 1886
The Oise Book of Pile-Drivers—H. Longuevélo, 1887
The Oise Book of Water-Butts—G. Veuseveute, 1888
Journal Médical Français, 1889, Vol. XIII, pp. 123–135